WITHDRAWN

D1311009

Without Dividend In Mind

Epigrams and Easy Essays

Text by J. Vincent Hansen

Wood Engravings by Claire Leighton

NORTH STAR PRESS OF ST. CLOUD, INC.
St. Cloud, Minnesota

I.SBN: 978-0-87839-822-5

Printed in the United States of America by Sentinel Printing.

Published by
North Star Press
P.O. Box 451
St. Cloud, MN 56302

www.northstarpress.com

To Vincent
for reminding me
what the world needs fewer of
is *normal* people.

". . . when a man has not lived for himself alone, but has transformed his vitality into deeds and ideas which have passed into the consciousness of others — then it is not so easy to know when to pronounce him dead."

Marcia MacDermott
The Apostle of Freedom

All birth is alike, while death is made various by the interim vows.

EASY ESSAY CCXXIV

It is ours to add to the world's ledger a column for those things the heart need account for.

Easy Essay LXI

for Sebastian

Seek for yourself a friend
who would remind you
of the unwritten laws,
the sins of omission
and what was not said.

EASY ESSAY CCXXXII

Pity was never meant to be squandered on the naked, hungry, and homeless but rather held in reserve for those unable to imagine themselves likewise.

for Sylvester Brda

Love was never intended
to be wholesaled as a verb,
but rather retailed as a noun.

EASY ESSAY CLXVII

for Jeanette and Joan

While the World is about having to do something big, Love is about choosing to do something small.

Easy Essay CCXXVI

for Vincent and Carly

In the movements of those
the World deems slow
resides liturgy, and in their
silence, homily.

Holiness sustains itself
on the toll it exacts
from Sameness.

EASY ESSAY CLIV

If you have everything you
want, I will assume you
have but little, for it is not
in Want's nature to satisfy
in two places.

Eye and light are no match
for what it is that soul and
darkness manage.

What possible value could our second gift have where it is that listening was not the first?

Gentleness is balm
for all living things.

EASY ESSAY CLXI

As surely as *Yes* will
make its way from the
shade, *No* can be traced to
the one who planted the tree.

We get to name our silence
– Courage or Cowardice.

EASY ESSAY CCXIII

Even Silence and Music
are envious of the words
spoken on behalf
of the voiceless.

EASY ESSAY CCX

for Wendell Berry

By none are we served
better than the paranoia
informing the good steward
that he is being followed.

Easy Essay CCLII

with the Amish in mind

The meager light that
remains in a dark time
can always be traced to
the sense-tied as they
tend to an old fashion.

EASY ESSAY CCLXII

Ours is
a bloat of indulgence —
a malady born of sustained
affluence, marked by spillage,
blind optimism, and the
Pollyannaish assumption that
the bottom will never come
into view.

EASY ESSAY CCXLIV

Necessity,
Responsibility,
and Fidelity —

by these twined
we are bound.

EASY ESSAY VI

for August Preusser

To make a thing well, to be steward, to shun luxury and to remain indifferent to fashion, these are the cornerstones of conservation.

for Thomas More
(1478–1535)

Nature does not enter
the fray with so small
a weapon as opinion.

Easy Essay XLVIII

We are implicated by our very humanity, and to ever accept the *status quo* is to forever forgo our option to plead innocent.

Those who doubt God's goodness ought dwell on the fact that He based reality on our actions and not on our thoughts.

Easy Essay CCXIX

We are no two tested alike —
a corner post will give way in
the same soil where the line
post will hold.

Easy Essay LIV

Pride is the bureaucrat of
the soul that will employ a
hundred euphemisms where
there is but honest work
for a single word.

Sweat is the liquid
best known for putting
out theory.

EASY ESSAY LXXXVII

for George Pallansch

We ought listen carefully
for the words that find
employment in the wake of
honest sweat, for here it is
that another has winnowed
on our behalf.

EASY ESSAY CCXXXIX

Justice with all her muscle
can merely pay a debt, whereas
Mercy can forgive it.

for Dorothy Day

You will know Love,
for hers is a garment
of a fabric that has
fallen from fashion.

EASY ESSAY LII

How often we rejoice in the falling of another when we ourselves did not stake out a place sufficiently high to allow for the same possibility.

for Edward Barthel

He is of noble form
that would collaborate
with worm.

Easy Essay CLXXVIII

While Concrete remains
indifferent, Earth meets Rain
three buttons already undone.

Science can tell us
what empty is but not
why it hurts so bad.

EASY ESSAY CCXXXI

How insidious is the message we send to our children by our insistence on living as if there were no tomorrow?

Solitude is but fuel for a love that will not leave us alone.

EASY ESSAY CXLVI

for Fyodor Dostoyevsky
(1821–1881)

To say a thing that will yet
stand a hundred years out —
this the book owes the tree.

Easy Essay xxx

Capitalism ought come with
a warning label that would
caution one to the likely
hardening of heart, as the
one on Socialism would to
the inevitable loss of soul.

EASY ESSAY XVII

There always seems to be a lot more of *ours* when somewhere along the line it was called *mine*.

Easy Essay LXXVIII

for John Nix

The one unable to buy a
second shirt is poor,
while the one who gives away
his second shirt is rich.

With the exception of those who die in California, we too readily assume that the deceased in in a better place now.

Easy Essay CXXX

The common thief prowling
about under darkness
concedes more to truth
than does his fellow citizen
cloaked in majority burgling
at midday.

Easy Essay CXXXI

How foolish we are to
settle for Possession and
her meager nine-tenths,
when Appreciation long
ago agreed to grant us
the whole.

Easy Essay CXXXIX

To invest
in the continuity
of Truth and Beauty
without dividend in mind—
this is portfolio
of the highest kind.

Easy Essay CCLXIII

for Damien of Molokai
(1840–1889)

Love does not squander her
time where her absence
would mean one fewer, but
instead, goes to the place
where it would spell alone.

Ode to leisure

Time was so much easier
to find before it became
money.

Easy Essay CCVII

for Paul Fagan &
Herb Gappa

We are not called on to entertain *the glass half empty or half full;* our charge is with the empty glass and the one running over.

for Ralph Dehler

Well shaped
the calloused hand is
for holding answer.

EASY ESSAY XCIII

Competition is that
conflicted creature that
will award with fanfare
to the winner a worthless
trophy, and then later
under darkness, onto the
loser, bestow a thing of
great value.

Should it come to a vote –
Love has already failed.

EASY ESSAY CCXXII

for Al & Clara Schreifels

Ritual and routine are the arms of Time that promise to hold us in good stead.

EASY ESSAY CLXIV

For Modernity to advance,
she must first strafe with
humor all things Holy.

EASY ESSAY V

Of the one who does not
tramp off in pilgrimage to
modernity's shrines —
perhaps it is that his Soul
was not invited by its
architects.

Easy Essay clix

for Jean-Francois Millet
(1814–1875)

While the artist does not
know what he is doing, he
consoles himself with the
knowledge that his
ignorance is but the husk
of a thing yet to be seen.

Where rain ruined the day —
I suspect the day.

EASY ESSAY XLIII

The acoustics of affluence
do not allow us to hear
what it is the things we
own say about us.

Easy Essay CCIII

Charity ought not be
about the end and our
accountant but rather the
beginning and our brother.

Easy Essay CXV

From History a sense of
debt, from debt a sense of
gratitude, and from gratitude
a sense of humility—

minus these we are
destined to perpetual
adolescence.

Fear is the thumb that clinches the fist of bigotry.

Easy Essay XVI

We vaccinate our children
for measles and pox; then
prop them in front of a
television — as if mere dew
could hurt them in a way
that a raging flood could
never.

Easy Essay CCLXI

The World's limp cannot be traced to the little lies we squander on each other, but rather to the big ones we tell ourselves.

EASY ESSAY CCLIV

Of this new Church,
wherein God has been
replaced by *A Majority*
and *Harris* and *Gallup*
fill out its Trinity —

might we never find
ourselves in its pews.

EASY ESSAY CCXI

Forward and backward
are the movements of a
secular dance that can only
be redeemed by upward.

EASY ESSAY CCXXXVIII

Avoid always those who
use tithing like a carpenter
would a dull chisel; as if
Jesus could enter Calcutta
with one hundred dollars in
his cloak and exit clutching
ninety.

for Louie Hanauska

A good man will give away his second coat; a holy man, his favorite.

Easy Essay CCXXXII

for Hannah

My hope for you, child,
is that there will always
remain a place for you to go
where knowledge has yet
to put out awe.

It is between
seeing and naming
that joy flickers.

EASY ESSAY XX

Time and the World conspire
to insure that only children
can know happiness. Later
on, should we remain simple,
we get a shot at joy, and
the sophisticated must settle
for being amused on occasion.

Noise has a hundred spokesmen while Silence speaks for itself.

Easy Essay LXXXIII

So much is made of our
choices now. But remove what
offends the eye, grates on
the ear and insults the
mind, and we awake beside
our brother in Bangladesh.

Affluence is the hostess
unable to find a way
to make us comfortable
without leaving us lapsed.

EASY ESSAY CLXII

From Enough there is
a road that leads to More
and a path that leads
to Less.

Easy Essay XXXV

Apathy is always forced
to entertain guests that she
cannot recall having invited.

EASY ESSAY XV

for Lawrence Omman

Deep down Soil is an old-fashioned girl who demands a long courtship followed by a church wedding.

Easy Essay VII

Stay clear always of those who would confuse equality with justice: those who cannot view the Grand Canyon without wishing to stuff Mount Everest into it.

My Creed

for Julius Two-Hearts,
Zele Madulingi &
Xiao Dong Wei

I will savor all my brothers
and sisters — red, yellow, black
and brown — and not let
the world wring from me the
utterance: *I am colorblind,*
and with it the inference
that the greatest Artist of
all somehow erred.

for Robert Cashin

A friend is a place
to pull over for our
soul's sake.

EASY ESSAY CCXXXVII

I have seen evil up close
and sometimes it was Satan
himself; other times merely
Faith trying to carry on in
Charity's absence.

If we do not have enough, perhaps it is because we did not give enough away.

EASY ESSAY CXXXIV

for Angeline Workman

As to my own journey and
heroes, the truth cannot
keep oddness at bay, for
mostly they were women
and none in uniform.

Easy Essay CCLVI

for Mary Ann Siebels

The good that one does
times the number of people
in the world ought equal
enough to go around.

It is *theology* not *technology* that determines the size of the world.

Easy Essay CCXXIII

If we would settle for
knowing, we ought pay our
tuition and get on with it;
but if our need is to
understand, then we must
enroll ourselves at the feet
of the tired.

Easy Essay CLXXVI

Every bit as precious as
the love that enables us to
forgive, is the work that
allows us to forget.

EASY ESSAY CCXLIII

for Joe and Emily Brda

Where the proud hold all
by the handle of certainty –
the humble grip mystery.

The one who claims to have gotten the last word understands silence least.

for Katie Wruck

Love does not arrive at the
finish standing tall, for bent
is the posture of caring.

Easy Essay CCXLI

for Frank & Marina

More than from books
I took from the quiet lives
that spoke volumes.

Easy Essay CCCVII

Is there another among us
half so difficult to be near
as the one unaware that
something very precious
has been lost?

The silence of the Old can be traced to their knowledge of what tomorrow will erase.

Easy Essay li

To miss Spring is never
to have played; to miss
Summer is never to have
labored; to miss Autumn is
never to have suffered;
and to miss Winter
is not possible.

Easy Essay cli

for Marcella Hoffmann

Of the Innocence that manages its way to the finish – it is no waste of our time to inquire of its journey.

Easy Essay CCII

Where the traveler
is pilgrim; his movement,
liturgy; and his promise,
vow – hope remains.

Easy Essay CCIX

While a portion of Progress
remains in going forward,
who would argue now that
the better part does not
reside in returning?

Easy Essay CCXXI

A Blessing it is to arrive
at the end with no debt
but to him whose weight
slowed us down.

Acknowledgements

Even a work as terse as this manages to usher in debt. I have need to thank David Leighton for his making available the precious wood engravings of his aunt, Claire Leighton (1898-1989).

Thank you, Peter Maurin (1877-1949), long-time friend of Dorothy Day, whose idea Easy Essays first was.

Thank you to Corinne Dwyer, friend and editor, for always being at the other end of the phone.

And as always, to my wife, Jeanette, who teaches me daily of the quiet nature of selflessness.